SPLINTERS OF LIGHT

*Without the support of Cristina this book would not have
seen a splinter of light.* JK

For Heddy, Julius and Feri with love. JL

*This book is dedicated to William, Will, Juliette and my
parents Charles and Lena, thanking them for all their love
and support.* JP

*For all the splinters of my life perhaps this book will be the
healing plaster.* RT

SPLINTERS OF LIGHT

Johannes Kerkhoven
Judy Langton
Jean Pestell
Rosanna Taylor

Published by
HIGHWOOD HOUSE PUBLISHING

First published in this edition in 2004
by
HIGHWOOD HOUSE PUBLISHING
Highwood House 31 Hampstead Lane Highgate Village
London N6 4RT

All rights reserved
Copyrights © remain with the authors

ISBN 0-9546716-0-0

Printed and Bound By
JRDigital Print Services Ltd Whitstable KENT CT5 3QY

Contents

In Praise of Plumpness	JK	7
The Visitor	–	8
This Side of Last Week	–	9
Temptation – Please	–	10
The Old Tilba Road	JL	11
Sydney Summer	–	11
Transience	–	12
Love Lost	–	12
Evening	–	12
Childhood	–	13
Oh, Baby	–	13
The Travelling Group	–	14
Blind Man	–	14
The Other Side of the Wall	–	15
Question	JP	16
On a Canal in France	–	16
Ripples	–	17
Witness	–	17
Clouds Like Roses	–	18
Somewhere	–	18
Brief Encounter	–	19
Discretion	–	19
From Bury Hill	–	20
Humming Bird	–	20
Garden Philosophy	RT	21
London Town	–	22
Housel Bay, Cornwall	–	23
Eleven Days	–	24
Enemy Lines	–	25
Esplanade	JK	26
Discretion	–	27
Mary	–	28
The Snail	–	28
Fcuk	–	29
Spitfire	–	30
Bank Holiday	JL	31
The Waiting Room	–	31
Autumn on Hampstead Heath	–	32
Winter	–	32
Journey	–	33
The Nursing Home	–	33
Venice	–	34
St. Petersburg	–	34
Writer's Block	–	35
The Dinner Party	–	35
Cannibal	JP	36
The Known Soldier	–	36

contents continued

Moonlight	JP	37
Dead Sea	–	37
Kingley Vale	–	38
Niagara	–	39
TV America	–	40
Familiar Face	RT	41
Angelus Bells	–	42
Modern Dilemma	–	43
Aftermath	–	44
Beyond Memory	–	44
Inky-Beer	–	45
In Bricks We Trust	JK	46
Cycles	JL	47
Beach on Goa	JP	48
Eclipse	–	49
Cat	RT	50
Skulls	JK	51
Hysterical Laughter	–	52
Hello Dad	–	53
Choice	–	53
Three Short Poems	–	54
Dreams	JL	55
Sleep	–	55
Memories	–	56
Re-birth	–	56
Afterthoughts	–	57
Memorial	–	57
The Condor	JP	58
A Winter's Morning	–	59
Family Reunion	–	60
Even When	RT	61
Flowers	–	61
Is there more....	–	62
55 Springs	–	63
Notes on Contributors		64

Acknowledgements

Some of these poems first appeared in the following publications:

JK — **Blossom** and **Walk** appeared in *In the Company of Poets.* **Blossom** also appeared in *Connections* **In Praise of Plumpness** and **Temptation Please** in *Literary Review.*

JP — Bury Hill in *The West Sussex Gazette* .

JOHANNES KERKHOVEN

In Praise of Plumpness

For me no skinny little frump
with bones like dagger points.
Give me a lady who is plump
with smoothly covered joints.

I can't resist a dimpled knee,
and firm pink cheeks and lips.
A silky-soft skin, that's for me,
all over ample hips.

Ah! Rubens' ladies; what delight,
big-breasted, bare and bold.
Keep Lowry's matchsticks out of sight,
there's nothing there to hold.

Thin feels like half of her's not there.
Plump's *always* gorgeous, clothed or bare.

The Visitor

walking
straight-
backed
sleek
as a
silver birch
a good
golden
head
taller
than I

legs
moving
with
the serious
regularity
of a
long
pendulum

aubergine
cheeks
in tandem
inside
her Levis

slowly

l e f t -

r i g h t -

l e f t -

r i g h t
she
passes me
effort-
lessly
smoothly
gliding
on
scented oil
looking
neither
left
nor right

sublime
irresist-
ible
ethereal

real?

This Side of Last Week

You walked past me in The Strand;
touch-close,
your face, faun-like,
gilded by the afternoon sun.
Intent, you failed to notice me.
There in a flash
love's bitter-sweet and burning sting—
long lost,
was back.
Ah, I thought, if only I could be
that soft sweet breeze
caressing your beloved face.

Temptation – Please

I'm cool with young mothers, don't curse them like others,
when I have to jump clear of a pram.
I don't spit in the street and prefer not to cheat
and would certainly never say 'damn'.

If I do break a cup, I will always own up,
and then offer to clean up the mess.
If you spilled some red wine on white trousers of mine
I would smile and demand no redress.

We know cats are quite thick, but when mine needs a kick
I relent and will give it a stroke.
I've stopped biting my nails and now only drink ales.
I'll help anyone who's broke.

So dear Lord, you can tell that I've done rather well.
My behaviour's been better than best.
So dear Lord if you're there and dear Lord if you care,
may I proffer a tiny request?

It's not money I need, I don't know the word greed
but I don't like feeling frustrated.
If you could fit me in, would you please make me sin?
I'd be much obligated.

Yes, send me temptation and such titillation
that I will be rapacious with lust.
Being saintly can wait, at a hundred-and-eight
man can still raise a trifle of thrust.

JUDY LANGTON

The Old Tilba Road

Cracked bitumen remembering
the whirl of passing cars;
a deserted path
between ocean and wetlands.

Marsh tern, black swan,
white ibis, dusky moor hen
on glass-still water.

The ocean thunders
onto seamless sand.
A lone jogger wanders by.

Earth and sky touch infinity.

Sydney Summer

Gum trees whisper secret codes.
Cicadas drone their empty song.
Boats bob on harbour
in syncopated dance.

Harsh sun wrinkles my face.
Ice cold mangoes
by the swimming pool.

Humidity numbs my mind.

Transience

Why do flowers
give me so much pleasure?

They fade and die
like your bewitching smile
that I still remember.

Love Lost

I lost you.

Shadows linger.
Thoughts unspoken,
dreams unfulfilled.

Love lost before its time.

Evening

Soft light falls on tired faces,
air is touched by frost.
I am saddened by traces
of dear ones I have lost.

Childhood

Skipping, playing
useless braying.
Noughts and crosses,
snakes and ladders.
Hours of leisure,
endless pleasure.

Innocence on a wing,
rebukes that sting.
Halcyon days
of sunshine, flowers.
Broken toys, unmade beds
and secret sheds.

Oh, Baby

Oh, baby
cocooned in your pram
awash with sleep,
I watch you in awed silence.

Swaddled in your dreams
you do not hear birds sing,
or the rustle of leaves.
The cacophony of conflict
passes you by.

Dream baby
as long as you can.

The Travelling Group

We meet each other;
judging, assessing,
breaking silence,
cracking jokes.

Alliances form, break down,
opinions alter.
Insecurity drives some,
others withdraw.

At the end
a sense of loss,
of sadness.

Even transient friends
are valuable.

Blind Man

He was blind.
Wore the affliction lightly,
eschewing a dog.
His wife a constant shadow
steering him through life.

His courage enhanced my holiday,
a zest for life
that took my breath away.

The Other Side of the Wall
(A view from East Berlin)

The wish for freedom
a gnawing ache.
To scale the unscaleable,
walk unfettered
not fearing the chilling knock.
Travel to forbidden places,
write the unthinkable
breathe and not be afraid of breath.

The Wall fell,
not as we had dreamed.
Untethered capitalism,
corruption, greed
stalked the streets.
Illusions shattered like brittle glass.
Disappointment fermented
like rotting compost.

The soured face of freedom.

JEAN PESTELL

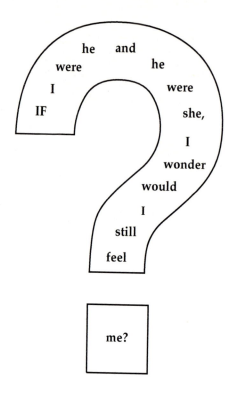

On a Canal in France

Water linking landscapes,
odours stretching senses,
creamy fragrance,
fuelling summer pleasures.

Loving friendships,
wrapped in endless laughter,
creating bonds
in the preparation.

Ripples

A pebble
thrown into a pond,
ripples spread out and out.

Once calm water,
reflecting normal sun
and trailing clouds,
marbled now.

Ever increasing circles,
their effect reverberates,
moving in relentless bands
toward the final dark circle.

Now the pond is still,
only reflections have changed.

Like love,
every ripple felt.

Witness

I searched for you today
in white-edged winter,
amid the grief of others.

I found the place
you share in troubled soil.
Black earth which you enrich
supports your rose in solemn pose:
cut back, naked, hard pruned.
Wicked thorns stab the memory,
icicles bleed from my occluded heart,
witness again to so much sorrow.

I felt your hand move
with vultures of wind,
coax out my inner words,
slide along my lips
as I called your name.

I hope you heard.

Clouds Like Roses

Clouds like roses,
winged and wafting
on a favoured wind.

Softly spooled petals
damask bright,
curled in the canopy.

Crumpled white tissue roses,
buds flecked with sulphur tints,
float in a cerulean sky.

A sliding Venus sun's brush strokes
paint a roseate glow,
smudge the red eye of day.
Chiffon shadows mirrored in lakes,
and the last rain that fell.

Clouds like roses bloom unscented,
pierced by thorns of sunlight,
now blood red in the shrinking sky:
a wreath on the canvas.

Clouds like roses,
nature's bouquet we gather with our eyes.

Somewhere

I am somewhere, in the middle of nowhere:
here, in a place not on any map or plan.

Where it is doesn't matter, I do not care,
I am somewhere, in the middle of nowhere.

All I know is that healing waters flow there,
cleansing the outer and inner man.

I am somewhere, in the middle of nowhere:
here, in a place not on any map or plan.

Brief Encounter

Was it you I saw buying saucy undies?
It certainly looked like you in the queue.
Funny, your wife said you worked Mondays.
Well, maybe it wasn't you.

It certainly looked like you in the queue,
although you seemed quite agitated,
well, maybe it wasn't you.
We could have chatted if you'd waited.

Although you seemed quite agitated,
has your wife lost that much weight?
We could have chatted if you'd waited,
is she really a 10 or an 8?

Has your wife lost that much weight?
I thought I noticed a gleam in your eyes.
Is she really a 10 or an 8:
you certainly knew her new size.

I thought I noticed a gleam in your eyes,
funny, your wife said you worked Mondays.
You certainly knew her new size.
Was it you I saw buying saucy undies?

Discretion

Petticoat of leaves,
hoisted up against smooth pines.
Earth sighs with pleasure,
undressed and ready for spring.
Discreet snow has crept away.

From Bury Hill

Nesting birds spread
wings devouring blue.
Below, lakes
and ponds distort pathways,
contours mocked.
Across safe fields firm hands
broadcast seed, wind
and insects adorn the land
in wild frocks.

Bold, vermilion warm sun
genuflects to
soft clouds.
Relentless beauty marked
indelibly
by homesteads, skulking low
to charm the tranquil
pinewoods, bird song hushed
in reed-beds. Close, water meadows full
of summer joy.

Humming Bird

Let's celebrate life with the humming bird
as it hovers for syrup around the tree.
Overhead, hawks cry out to be heard,
let's celebrate life with the humming bird,
with every action, with every word,
sip the nectar, fly and be free,
let's celebrate life with the humming bird
as it hovers for syrup around the tree.

ROSANNA TAYLOR

Garden Philosophy

Isolated cries of a hungry bird
broken by a sudden rush of wing
parallel my early morning awakening:
the same reason why my heart begins to sing.

Companionably, we eye each other.
I dripping sleep and tea, dig the ground;
he, gaze severely trained, waits patiently
to relieve the startled worm from its warm mound.

In a cameo of silence, I stop, take breath,
watch him bravely break cover,
dart and dive, carry away his life-giving prize.
One good turn deserves another.

But what of the worm in all this:
aerator of soil, what is his gain?
Ah, in the pursuit of grace we must accept our place.
It is his fate to be the lowest in the food chain.

London Town

We rode on London trolley-buses
     paying pennies for our fares,
we roamed its many bombsites
     and played upon its squares.
The single tickets on the buses
     were rainbow colours then;
collecting them with holy fervour,
     to compare them in our den.
We strutted down its Soho streets
     drinking in the Latin theme,
a wondrous vibrant place to be in -
     a space in which to dream :
two children looking in the window
     of life so different there;
the mandatory Sunday visit
     to St. Patrick's in the Square.
Our mothers used to send us
     to the corner shop to buy
the things that they'd forgotten
     and we'd willingly comply;
we'd skip along the empty road
     without a worried thought
and trundle back, no traffic-jam
     delayed us with what we'd bought.
They asked us to go buy cigarettes
     in the local tobacconist:
'Old Man George' would frighten us
     with cigar, red-wig and fist.
On rainy days, a special treat
     the British Museum was first choice;
we'd play hide'n'seek, run round guards.
     Without making any noise
we'd scamper up the marble staircase
     to the magic Egyptian Rooms,
dare one another to look at 'Ginger'
     then tour its catacombs.
What fun we had, my cousin and I:
     in those halcyon yesterdays;

we'll not forget the time of youth
       now we're further in life's maze.
And though we live out on the fringe
       we often go back down -
re-visit the streets, the shops, the squares
       of our lovely London Town.

Housel Bay, Cornwall

Sitting on the edge of the land,
sea-mist clouding my expectant view;
tide high: cold, deep and grey;
life on hold, clasping in my hand,
a perfect moment, shared with you,
I slowly merge into the day.

The ephemeral mist lifts, falls again,
thunder voices its loud majesty;
lightning, its wanton power.
A screen of wild electric rain
draws us closer: you're touching me.
Horizon peeps between the shower.

Listening to wind cry, storm beating on,
descending dark spreads pervading gloom.
Warm, dry, together, breathing low,
an audience, heartbeats as one,
in an insignificant room
we watch Nature get on with her show.

Eleven Days

Within the walls of my world
I leave my comfortable house,
car-riding the short distance
to shop for my family.
I need the boot for the overflowing plastic bags.

As bombs dropped,
you sheltered, unprepared,
in the cellar
under your high-rise block for
eleven days.

The supermarket is full.
I pause at the bakery.
The mountain of cellophaned bread fascinates me.

In your shelter, you had bread
for eight days
but not
eleven.

No longer certain of the safety
of tap water, I look at the long aisle
of plastic bottled waters that
come from near and far.

In that cellar, you had water
for nine days
but not
eleven.

Enemy Lines — *for my Croation cousin*

A cigarette
never leaves her fingers,
ash falls unheeded;
her face, haloed
by the bluegrey floating smoke,
is a spectre of its former self.

Shared teenage
dreams and hopes,
long since stored
but not forgotten,
litter our different paths.

Since I last saw her,
enemy lines have etched
across that once smooth face,
like a river networking
its tributaries of lace
deep into the land.

Her laughter,
once impetuous,
so infectious, has muted
to a wry smile that does not
spread to her eyes.

Clasping her hand,
I feel the lack of youth
in the sandpaper skin;
see the yellow-ochre stain
has reached the nails
once painted war-paint
colours of fashion.

With the voice
of an old woman
she says,
"Don't tell me about smoking.
Tell me what's
been happening to you
these last 5 years...."

JOHANNES KERKHOVEN

Esplanade

lightly planted
on the hard BENCH
milk-eyes aim at the sea

        not   seeing
children dancing in his mind

skip ping   laughing

          slipping

leaping   yester   day

        into   today

dog jumping   licks

        now
        he turns
the face   away
breaks
  i
  n
  t
  o
a smile   showing remaining teeth

        the breeze lifts

hunched   a white wisp of hair
shoulders
     shiver seagulls scr-e-e-e-ch

aching
     limbs s t r — e — t c h
he stands
     joints c r e a k
he looks
     ◀ left and right ▶
damn!   where am I
     where is she?

Discretion

Discretion is no part of Valerie
and all of her is ice.
Her lips are sharp as razorblades,
her legs a human vice.
The very worst of ev'rything
she turns men into mice.
She'll whip and slash and torture you
with every known device.

She takes delight in hurting you,
it gives her life its spice.
And Valerie gives to her best friends,
the clap, the pox and lice.
She always without warning
will quote, then up her price.
Be careful when she feels you,
she might cut off a slice.

When if you're feeling lonely
you buy her merchandise
and feel you're being wicked,
boy, will you pay the price!
And if you've lost your heart to her
(could happen in a trice),
you're lost, you're gone, your history,
you're human sacrifice.

Valerie is sugar and vice
she's bitter-sweet
for any budding masochists
she is the end-all treat.

Mary

Mary had a little man
his hair was white as snow
and every time he tried his luck
he got a mighty blow.

Mary said as he fell down,
'That gave me quite a thrill.'
So when he scrambled to his feet
she hit him harder still.

Mary thought, I'll break his neck,
and moved in for the kill.
Because she knew the silly goat
had put her in his will.

The Snail

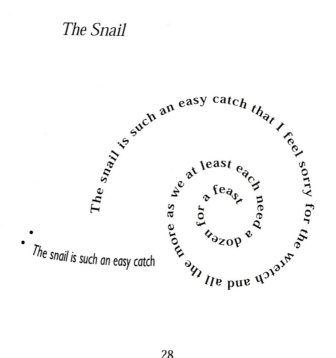

The snail is such an easy catch that I feel sorry for the wretch and all the more as we at least each need a dozen for a feast

• The snail is such an easy catch

FCUK!!

FCUK!!

FCUK!!

FCUK!!

LOEV
COTIUS
POCULATE
FCUKING
ecretion
hradon
gavina
citloris
pirck
pneis
psusy
cnut
dcik
srecw
fcuk
moce
ograsm

LUNNI-
CINGUS
TELLA-
FIO

TINER-
COURSE
EXSUA-
LITY

Spitfire

I bombed railway stations,
two oil installations,
until they were totally flat.
I felt such elation
at their devastation,
I felt like a god doing that.

I shot down three fighters
and cheered as the blighters
burned up like a firework display.
I was decorated,
fêted
for blowing those devils away.

Of course, that's all done now,
life's not *that* much fun now;
I just drive this silly old bus.
I use all my nerve now
to start, stop and swerve now
and threaten old fogeys that fuss.

I love kicking off louts
and half-pissed down and outs,
I terrorise cars out of habit.
If some fool wants to pass me
or try to outclass me
I'll soon have him meek as a rabbit.

I frighten all hikers
unsaddle bikers
laugh while they curse in the rough.
I send everyone flying
just short of dying.
I feel then I'm doing my stuff.

JUDY LANGTON

Bank Holiday

My footsteps echo on cavernous paths
in eerie silence with no laughs.
Empty cars sit mute with
secrets of owners
no longer there.

The currawong* cries in pain;
there has been no rain
for some time.
A lone cyclist hisses by
giving the lie
to stillness.

I linger in the balmy air
wrapped in thoughts
I will not share.

*Currawong is an Australian bird that emits
a plaintive call.

The Waiting Room

The smell of wetness and smoke
chokes the air,
scrunched-up debris litters
the floor.
A dim light blinks onto
graffiti-stained walls.

Two prim nuns sit oblivious
of squalor.
An elderly man buried
in The Times.

I join them shattering
their silence, dripping
from incessant rain.

Autumn on Hampstead Heath

A burnished carpet scrunches underfoot
while floating leaves dance above my head.
Watery sun barely melts the clouds.

Ducks quack in abject space,
swans glide on silent drift.
A stillness grips the air.

The threat of winter
creeps into my soul.

Winter

Rotting leaves
speckle streets.
Footsteps slosh
wet pavements.
Umbrellas dance
above flying hair.

Naked trees
twist in a bleak sky.
Chill winds
seize my bones.

The long arm of winter
grips me by the throat.

Journey

A strange face
reflected in the mirror
unknown in my youth.

Stiffness
accompanies my movements.
Memory dips and spins.

The joy of wasted hours–
immersed in music
bewitched by theatre
entwined in a novel.

A new sense
of freedom reigns.

The Nursing Home

They sit waiting
aching with nothingness.
Visitors staunch the stench
of loneliness.

Empty hours filled with
machine-like precision;
breakfast, lunch, dinner.
In between, television
blankets the rest.

Waiting for death.

Venice

Endless crowds
shuffle along the Rialto.
Heat and pollution;
yet nothing dims
the magic of this jewel.

Gondolas slither along
canals at dusk.
Elegant palaces echo
to foreign feet.

A floating theatre-set
of romantic dreams.

St Petersburg

Like a down-at-heel woman,
pockmarked and ravaged.

Grandly planned boulevards
bisect soulful rivers.

Dazzling and obscene opulence,
rooms smothered in gilt.

Beggars open gnarled hands,
broken in body and spirit.

People in limbo,
lost in a sea of change.

Writer's Block

Crippled thoughts,
ink is dry.
I don't know why.

Give the muse
time to return.
The creative urge
will burn.

Let cinders settle,
a spark will glow—
words should flow.

The Dinner Party

A social construct
of no great pleasure,
I have better things
to do with leisure.

Idle chit-chat
to strange faces,
inept laughter
in all the wrong places.

The meat is burnt
the sweet is rotten,
no wonder the event
is best forgotten.

JEAN PESTELL

Cannibal

He devoured her on the back seat
of his car parked in a side street.
He'd preferred someone much younger,
but to satisfy his hunger
took the first one who seemed willing,
who'd accepted the King's Shilling.

She had certainly egged him on
by her injudicious beckon-
ing. Here she was ripe for the feast,
her loud cries excited the beast.
Pink flesh succumbed in pure delight
as he prepared for the first bite.

Sweet mound so soft and cavernous,
by now he was so ravenous.
She screamed out with delight,
but then he had an awful fright
as he prepared to quell his need.
Too late he realised that he'd
bitten off more than he could chew:
she was a cannibal too!

The Known Soldier

The chance to waste your time has gone.
Frivolity and fun gone, too.
Blown by the wind of death
those fragments of your life
are pieced together now in ours.

One young life sucked out,
kissed only by the wicked lips of war.
Here lies an almost lost love,
plucked from that deep relinquary of secrets.
It blooms, remembered in our freedoms:
freedom to live at will,
freedom to waste our time.

Moonlight

I am bathing in its glow.
Silver paints the inky night.
Does moonlight flow like water?

Does moonlight flow like water?
Silver paints the inky night.
I am bathing in its glow.

Dead Sea

No fishing boat
ever rocked here.

Iridescent sea,
dead to harvest,
closed to life.

Long salt collar
chokes the soft brown shore.
Intrepid bathers hug shallow depths.

Parched tongues of land
moulded by salt,
gasp in the heat.
Ripples on the weighty surface
spiral backwards.

Birds mark the edges
with sharp warning cries.

Kingley Vale

I

Long anguine chalk paths coil
around the ancient yews.
Thin white girdle scores the contours
of the darkly dense groves.

Impenetrable undergrowth,
light and noise extinguished,
haven to the smallest creatures
huddled in the reserve.

Furtive dormice, stoats and weasels
furrow black arteries.
Deer, badger cetes, skulking foxes
share deep unlit shadows.

Yews of the forest brace their limbs
against the centuries.
Cold shrill winds, strong storms pushed away;
a sanctuary preserved.

II

The fox
running lightly
down the porous spine,
turf undisturbed,
small heath grasses tremble,
dark woods weld together.

Brushing the long leather yew leaves,
their creamy linen underside
catching the only light.
Pungent wood sage fills the air:
the fox is in his kingdom.

Niagara

From dawn to dawn great teeming tresses fall:
relentless mane of water shears the days,
its constant force chisels the rock face wall,
dark contours vanish in a rolling haze.
Majestic river plunges without pause
across the weathered lip shaping its flow.
A floating shroud of mist spreads out like gauze
on deep mauve wounds in cauldrons far below.
Wild shards of blue dissolve in pools of green,
cascades of crystal spear each passing hour,
a veil of wayward wisps contains a scene
of flowing furrows generating power.

Departed sunsets glower in the blend,
we feel the thunder sweep us to the end.

Horseshoe Falls, Niagara

TV America   September 11 2001

'Breaking news: America under attack
Hi-jacked planes have hit the Twin Towers
Debris falling like snow on white and black
Casualties unknown for hours and hours

Hi-jacked planes have hit the Twin Towers
Terror has scarred the Land of the Free
Casualties unknown for hours and hours
A stain on the Statue of Liberty

Terror has scarred the Land of the Free
All States on maximum alert
A stain on the Statue of Liberty
The dead, the crying, the pain and the dirt

All States on maximum alert
The President declares it an act of war
The dead, the crying, the pain and the dirt
Nothing like this has happened before

The President declares it an act of war
Debris falling like snow on white and black
Nothing like this has happened before
Breaking news: America under attack '

ROSANNA TAYLOR

Familiar Face

Smiling eyes
shining out;
camera-posed
cheeky grin
complemented by
stylised hair.

An invitation to
"read the real story –
share my grief,
share my glory."

All your tastes:
likes and dislikes too.
I know everything –
sometimes even
before you do.

The Press builds you up,
pulls you down;
calls you icon,
calls you clown.

But the face I see
is one I know,
every contour,
every bone.

My feeling is
your face
is as familiar as
my own.

Angelus Bells

Once only nuns feet whispered here,
bare skin toughened on cool
pebbled steps, skirts swishing
like the moaning wind combing
through the leafy canopy.
Heads bent, lips in eternal prayer,
the clacking rosary beads mingling
with the wild calls of mating birds
drowned by the Angelus Bells
slicing through the noon heat.

Now the tourist snake climbs noisily,
feet well-shod, thirsty for the promised view.
Defiant geraniums, wilful bizzie-lizzies
splash shades of red, pink and white
in the green, while the high sun dapples through
whitening the blue and grey of the steps.

Sounds of the modern world
are left in abeyance.

My ears ache with anticipation:
Angelus Bells ring only in my head.

Modern Dilemma

Said mother to daughter, "I can't work this thing.
       I think I must be kind of dumb!
It stands in the corner, like little Jack Horner.
       When I'm near, I'm all fingers and thumbs!"

Said daughter to mother, "Don't worry, don't fear.
       It's really quite easy - don't fret!
I'll show you how. You'll learn in a flash.
       You'll soon see how good it can get."

Said mother to daughter, "There's too much to think of!
       My brain's very dead. You can see
I don't understand it. I'll never catch on.
       It's too clever, too modern, for me!"

Said daughter to mother, "You'll soon overcome it.
       If you like, I'll give you some time.
To make it much easier, I'll find a way
       of putting it down line by line.

First, switch the plug on, then press the big button
       WAIT, till the monitor clears!
The hard-drive is loaded, the key-board is ready.
       Click the icon, the programme appears."

"Click once on the icons? Sometimes it's double?
       Oh, daughter, it fills me with terror!
I don't think I've got it - I'm muddled already -
       I'm frightened of causing an error.

There's too many noises and beeps I'm not sure of.
       Please daughter, don't go away!
I need you beside me, to help and to guide me.
       I'll never learn this in a day!"

Said daughter to mother, "I'm sure you can do it.
       I'm off out. I can't stay at home.
My boyfriend is taking me out on the town.
       You'll have to manage it all on your own!"

Aftermath

Long after silence shatters eardrums
and dust is blinked from eyes;
long after heavy movement ceases
will survivors grasp their prize.

Will air breathe the more sweetly,
will the sky lose its fear
as destruction and the aftermath
engulf us far and near.

Oh, will victory be worth it,
can death outweigh the cost.
On balance will we be deserving
of embryonic talent lost.

Beyond Memory

You
sit in a corner of my mind
taking up unconscious space. Time
cannot keep still. It erodes my memory,
fills me with today, inevitably
pushing that last special meeting away
deep into my hardening heart.

Steps
of life become a sacred place
mirroring the missing parts. I cannot face
that you are beyond the place of memory.
Anniversaries matter to such as me
and with every forward step, it seems
the only place left for you, is in my dreams.

Inky-Beer

The kettle was singing a whistling song;
    the plates were all lining up.
Jigging a jig like an Irish doll
    the tray jumped into a cup.
        The cup was being filled, my dear,
          with a fountain of inky-beer, my dear,
          with a fountain of inky-beer.

The tea-towel was wiping its rolling eyes,
    not at all surprised, it seems,
at the knives and forks leaping like frogs
    cutting a cakeful of dreams.
        The cake was being filled, my dear,
          with a fountain of inky-beer, my dear,
          with a fountain of inky-beer.

The tea-spoons were tapping a tapping tune;
    the saucepans were acting bold.
Cleaning itself like a giant tom-cat,
    the oven blew hot and cold.
        The oven was being filled, my dear,
          with a fountain of inky-beer, my dear,
          with a fountain of inky-beer.

The scene was manic; over the top;
    everyone on the run.
Who do you think was pouring the beer?
    It was I creating the fun!
        It was I completely filled, my dear,
          with a fountain of inky-beer, my dear.
        It was I and a fountain of beer!

JOHANNES KERKHOVEN

In Bricks We Trust

JUDY LANGTON

Cycles

Rain drums on winter
windows in pitiless tune.
I wish there was snow.

Buds uncoil in spring,
lush green bewitches the eye.
New life awakens me.

Lazy summer heat
dulls the senses with perfumes.
Oh, what deep pleasure.

The melancholy
of autumn leaves drifting by.
Now I feel alone.

JEAN PESTELL

Beach on Goa

Hibiscus leads us to the beach,
a lure of life within our reach.
Paint brush palms, artily splayed, daub
the horizon as the great orb
of sun melts drifting ice-flow clouds,
dripping gold over thatched palm shrouds:
our shelters from the searing heat
while colours lap around our feet.

Last night's storm has reshaped the sand,
flat ochre acres deftly spanned
by glistening, golden fabric,
whose raw edges waves crimp and lick.
Miniature canyons form new banks,
undulating in sculpted ranks.
Unharnessed children shriek and call
as stirrups of sand break their fall.

Trenches of footprints surrender
to the tidal clock, as tender
lovers, hand from hand unravel,
startled by the foam or babble
from tides of beach vendors who press
their wares: silk sarongs, gaudy dress,
"Something new for your madam, sir,
colour very good, cheap for her."

Soft tea-leaf brown limbs, banyan strong,
urge and cajole, then move along.
Groups of joggers check pace and speed,
each pounded mile fulfilling need.
Wandering at a different pace,
sacred cows claim their holy space.
Countless dogs bark, swooping crows caw.
The sound of green bursts on the shore.

Eclipse

Sometimes I watch the moon at night
and remember the day
it blotted out the mighty sun.
Sudden darkness,
magical shadow bands over the sea.
Cosmic coincidence,
endless mystery.

Pilgrims in that moment,
witness to celestial majesty,
feeling the source of power weaken
as lowering clouds signalled the hour.

The alchemist moon,
specular, spectacular,
turned day into night
as the black spotlight
raced over us all,
enthralled, in thrall.

In awe, we saw
the momentous hand
of the complex Universe
sear our memories
in a velvet sky.

Excitement without fear,
joy without explanation.

Land's End, August 11, 1999.

ROSANNA TAYLOR

Cat

The cat sat on the mat.
His big round eyes glowed red.
The mat began to glow and grow.
Come fly with me, he said.

I stepped up on the mat.
We flew high in the sky.
I said goodbye to all I knew.
No time to think or cry.

I watched the world grow small.
Cat only looked at me.
We journeyed on, to a land, he said,
full of fun and harmony.

We cruised among the stars.
They lit up Cat and me,
brightening up the milky way.
The sky was made of tea.

The moon and sun bounced down,
together, stuck as one.
They rolled along the liquorice floor
and had all sorts of fun.

The trees dripped chocolate cake.
Their branches licked my face.
Spiders danced on golden silk,
spun candy-floss of lace.

Cat took me by the hand,
showed more lovely things.
Stay here, he said, and we can be
forever queen and king.

I said, I can't, you see:
you were too fast, too smart.
I had no time to pack a case -
I didn't bring my heart.

JOHANNES KERKHOVEN

<pre>
      S
   K U
      L
      L
      S
</pre>

gravediggers
pretending
to be
international
footballers

your grave
neatly tended
travelled with
me
in my mind

after

time
a n
opportunity
to   visit
say goodbye
once   again

He laughs
you're too
late   we

bought the plot for fifteen years

Hysterical Laughter

Ha! Ha! Ha! Ha! Ha! Ha! Ha! Ha!
Ha! Ha! Ha! Ha! Ha! Ha! Ha! Ha!
Ha! Ha! Ha! Ha! Ha! Ha! Ha! Ha!
Ha! Ha! Ha! Ha! Ha! Ha! Ha! Ha!
Ha! Ha! Ha! Ha! Ha! Ha! Ha! Ha!
Ha! Ha! Ha! Ha! Ha! Ha! Ha! Ha!
Ha! Ha! Ha! Ha! Ha! Ha! Ha! Ha!
Ha! Ha! Ha! Ha! Ha! Ha! Ha! Ha!
Ha! Ha! Ha! Ha! Ha! Ha! Ha! Ha!
Ha! Ha! Ha! Ha! Ha! Ha! Ha! Ha!
Ha! Ha! Ha! Ha! Ha! Ha! Ha! Ha!
Ha! Ha! Ha! Ha! Ha! Ha! Ha! Ha!
Ha! Ha! Ha! Ha! Ha! Ha! Ha! Ha!

Hello Dad

Among a thousand milling Russians
at St Petersburg railway station
I see my father,
standing next to the suitcase he inherited
from my grandfather.
He does not move or speak.
He recognizes me too and stares at me
for long intense seconds.
It is him all right, same hair, same pale skin,
same aquiline nose, same piercing eyes.

How did he manage to get here –
He's been dead twenty years.

Choice

You may consider biltong as a starter
smarter

I prefer the oyster
it's moister

Clerihew

Oedipus the King
did an awful thing,
killed his dad in a fit of road rage.
Then married his mum. Never asked her age.

Halfku

Ski like hell good sport
Après ski more good
Home without break bones best

Limerick

A man with one wife wanted more of 'em.
He decided to marry a score of 'em.
He said, I will be, if I'm right
on an average night
on speaking terms with at least four of 'em.

JUDY LANGTON

Dreams

Waves stir in my head.
Memories light up the screen
in illuminating segments.

Plots twist with my mood,
re-writing history.
Flying into pain and happiness.
An endless roundabout
of shifting images.

I wake to reality,
with relief and sadness;
another me.

Sleep

Elusive longing.
Velvety extinction
of daytime madness.
Drifting into inner peace.

Nightmares.
Emotions break the surface.

Tossing,
turning,
aching,
waking.

Sleep, oh sleep
bury me again.

Memories

Cherished memories of pain and pleasure
I retrieve from hidden caves of slow thought,
and look at each of them like lost treasure;
unlike ideas which can so easily be bought.

I catch myself dreaming of a past life
when joys and sorrows were part of each day,
and my being seemed without strife
for each precious moment was held at bay.

Walks in forests through a sea of bluebells,
the sun stroking our limbs like silken breath.
An enchantment of happiness that spells
the possibility of sudden death.

Now I try to no longer think of you
for the exquisite pain it puts me through.

Re-birth

The sun will shine,
weeds die.
I won't cry.

Crops will flourish,
grapes ripen.
My heart is open.

Love, a jewel
found in the wilderness
of my mind.

Afterthoughts

Hurts I inflicted
hurt me now.
Your aura is with me.

A control freak;
your inner core so shaky.
Strong facade
masked fragility.

The mystery of
misunderstanding
haunts our lives.

With your death
you and I are closer.

Memorial

Narrow claustrophobic corridor.
Visual brutality.

A white memorial Rose Garden
with plaques of regret and love.

Here I find tranquility.

I too will plant a rose
for a father I never knew.

JEAN PESTELL

The Condor

The hand of the mountain moves,
blots the image,
turns the river into a green vein,
sandstone pinnacles into temples of calm.

The escaping wind,
parched whistling lips,
moans through sun-struck cracks,
dissects landscapes like a whetted knife.

Scrubby plants squat,
small slits against the sky.
Stillness crowns the pines.

I fly on through unsuspecting day,
soar high and bank from rim to rim
into the glow of last light,
the river now obsidian black.

I am the condor,
time and isolation mine.

South Rim,
Grand Canyon

A Winter's Morning

The stalking full moon fades.
Early sun
claws veins in snow-starched fields.
Roof tiles,
plump as crusty loaves
sparkle in freshly-stacked rows.
Eager birds
slide along gutters,
to sip the melting drips.

A windless winter's day.
Twigs and branches
stiff with frost.
Leaves,
prisoners of the cold's slow release,
begin to stir.
Beyond,
pockets of white
puff up the apron of the hills.

Snug below the blanket,
brown threads of daily life,
rise on curves of land
rolled by centuries.

In pleached hedgerows
thrushes poke crooked shadows,
seeking ray-less depths for food:
ritual, speckled with darkness.
Worms still locked under solid earth
await the thaw.

Nearby, decaying windfalls lie:
gouged skulls around old apple trees.
Blackbirds fly to hornbeams,
tempted by the seeds
within lantern clusters of crystals.

Empty cold, full of life.

North Brewham, Somerset
New Year's Day 2002

Family Reunion

Profiles are the same,
a family name
   great grandparents shared.
It is to our shame,
we are all to blame,
   no-one knew or cared.

All our life styles bared,
see how each has fared
   further down the line.
Not a detail spared,
even wives compared,
   grapes from the same vine.

Meal time we are nine,
conversation fine,
   we're so glad they came,
laughter as we dine,
"Another glass of wine?"
   "Family!" we proclaim.

      Highgate Village, June 17, 2001

ROSANNA TAYLOR

Even When

I'll love you even when
the last of you has left my body
and you've become a stranger
in a familiar room;

even when your easy touch
and the impression of your lips
become a hazy memory;

and even when delirious dreams
leave my body empty,
then my imagination will still swell
and fill me with the ghost of you.

Flowers

Don't buy me hasty flowers;
     give me one hand picked with care.

Listen to my coded words.
     Laze beside me on the chair.

Pace the mountain by my side,
     match your footsteps as we walk.

Share the path, the hills, the valleys;
     stay on my side of the fork..

Encircle me with stubborn arms,
     contain me with your power.

Things once cut down, die all too soon.
     Leave fields to grow the flowers.

Is there more....

scrub the floor
     what does this mean
if I don't I can't be clean

dust the house
     vacuum the floor
is this all or is there more

do the ironing
     cook the meal
I think I'm starting not to feel

hang the washing
     darn the socks
six foot under in the box

but last night
     by the gate
we discussed the hand of Fate

the dancing stars
     showed the way
we have our lives we have a say

we have our souls
     we're not undone
the awakening has just begun...........

55 Springs

Laughter springs from deep inside,
regenerating a shallow soul.
55 springs I cannot hide:
laughter-lines are out of control.

Regenerating a shallow soul,
I hold on to youth to the very last.
Laughter-lines are out of control.
I realise now that summer's passed.

I hold on to youth to the very last;
no return to life's leisurely stroll.
I realise now that summer's passed;
loving and losing have made me whole.

No return to life's leisurely stroll,
summer's high noon has been and gone.
Loving and losing have made me whole.
Autumn's shadow falls fast and long.

Summer's high noon has been and gone.
Life springs into being at birth.
Autumn's shadow falls fast and long.
Being springs a fountain of worth.

Life springs into being at birth.
55 springs I cannot hide.
Being springs a fountain of worth.
Laughter springs from deep inside.

Johannes Kerkhoven was born in Holland, lived in Australia, 1954-79 and has lived in London since 1979. He is a happily retired compositor, graphic artist/photographer. His poems have been published in *Literary Review, Connections, Poetry 2000* anthology and *In the Company of Poets* anthology. He regularly performs his poetry and has been featured at Torriano and yearly with Poetic Licence, Upstairs at the Gatehouse Theatre, Highgate, London. He has published several short stories in Australia and the UK.

Judy Langton was born in Budapest, Hungary. At the age of seven she emigrated to Australia with her parents and younger sister. A graduate of *The National Institute of Dramatic Art* in theatre direction she began her career with The Melbourne Theatre Company. For many years she worked in theatre public relations both in Sydney and Melbourne. In 1983 she became a freelance arts journalist writing for *The Sydney Morning Herald* and *The Australian.* In 1985 she moved to England living in Sparsholt, a village near Winchester, where she continued writing, interviewing actors, directors and writers for the Australian newspapers and *The Times* in London.

Jean Pestell was educated in England and France. Trilingual, she worked at *Librairie Hachette* in London before moving to Spain where she taught English at *The British-American Institute* in Madrid, worked in radio, and was interpreter and publicist at the *Sevilla Film Studios.* In London she worked in the picture library for *Warner-Pathe,* before becoming a freelance photographer and archivist. She has for the past three years given public performances of her poems with Poetic Licence and has been published in *In the Company of Poets* and featured at the Torriano. Recently she inaugurated a cultural centre in Northern Goa, India and in 2003 appeared at the *Edinburgh Fringe Festival.*

Rosanna Taylor – a born and bred London Lover, cannot remember a time she did not write. From the age of seven when she realised that all those squiggly marks on the paper could be decoded she and her creative imagination were let loose. Currently writing a novel for children of some 50,000 words with sequels in the pipeline, she has also created a new colony of vampires from which a short story has been published in a Sci-fi magazine. Her poems have also been published in many Poetry pamphlets and she has read and appeared at the Torriano in Kentish Town, and yearly with Poetic Licence. Apart from the writing she has made and sold Dolls Houses and furniture in the past. Running synonymously with all this she is also an impassioned artist, has had exhibitions and sold all over the world.

Great Things

Level 10 – White

Helpful Hints for Reading at Home

The graphemes (written letters) and phonemes (units of sound) used throughout this series are aligned with Letters and Sounds. This offers a consistent approach to learning whether reading at home or in the classroom.

HERE ARE SOME COMMON WORDS THAT YOUR CHILD MIGHT FIND TRICKY:

water	where	would	know	thought	through	couldn't
laughed	eyes	once	we're	school	can't	our

TOP TIPS FOR HELPING YOUR CHILD TO READ:

- Encourage your child to read aloud as well as silently to themselves.
- Allow your child time to absorb the text and make comments.
- Ask simple questions about the text to assess understanding.
- Encourage your child to clarify the meaning of new vocabulary.

This book focuses on developing independence, fluency and comprehension. It is a white level 10 book band.

London Borough of Enfield	
91200000727847	
Askews & Holts	08-Sep-2021
JF YGN BEGINNER READE	
ENWINC	

Great Things

Written by
William Anthony

Illustrated by
Drue Rintoul

Chapter One

A Patch on One Eye

The sound of an engine rumbled along the forest floor. Voices whispered and were caught in the wind. The growl of the engine awoke another growl... a different growl. It was a growl from an animal. Two eyes twinkled in the dark.

The rumble came closer, before two bright lights lit up a family of tigers. The large tiger guarded two much smaller cubs. One cub had a large, round patch of black fur around its eye. The cubs backed away as their mother roared at the car. The car moved forward. So did the cubs' mother. A car door opened.

Roars and screams filled the forest. The two cubs scampered away as fast as their little legs could carry them.

One of the cubs found shelter inside a fallen log. It was all too much. The cub put its paws over its eyes. Hours passed, and night turned to day.

The cub opened its eyes as sunshine made its way into the log. It moved its paws slowly, one by one, before taking a nervous peep out of the end. The forest was silent.

Once it had built up enough courage, the cub made its way back home. Its mother and sister were nowhere to be seen. It tried to call, but its roar was more of a little meow.

The tiger searched for its mother and sister. Days, weeks and months went by. In fact, such a long time passed that the tiger was barely a cub anymore.

One day, the tiger's search led it somewhere very odd. The ground was hard and grey, and there were tall walls and lots of humans.

Chapter Two
Great Things

The shop bell tinkled as Darsha came in to stock up on paper. Darsha was only six, but she could craft anything with her little hands. She loved making things. Darsha also loved her name. It had a special meaning that said she would go on to do great things one day.

Darsha's eyes flicked between the green paper and the orange paper. Green was better for her dragon model, but orange was better for her paper fruit bowl. Green or orange? Dragon or fruit bowl?

"Everybody stay out of sight! Lock the door!" shouted a man as he burst into the shop, knocking off the bell.

The shopkeeper rushed to lock the door, while the shoppers hid behind stands and tables. Darsha curled up below the window. Screams from the street outside filled her ears. She moved up onto her knees and took a peep through the window. People were running and finding places to hide.

"Get down!" insisted the shopkeeper. Suddenly, the street fell silent.

Darsha didn't move. She was too curious. She stayed glued to the window.

The shoppers gasped.

A pair of eyes met Darsha's on the other side of the window. They were surrounded by orange, white and black fur, and underlined by long whiskers.

Darsha had never seen a tiger this close before. The tiger had never seen a human this close before either. But neither were scared. Darsha could see excitement in the tiger's eyes. The tiger looked playful and gentle. In one moment, the two seemed to have a connection. In the next, the tiger had dropped to the floor.

Chapter Three

Baagh Bhaee Bandhu

Two people grabbed the limp tiger and carried it towards a truck. As they loaded it on, Darsha noticed the words on the side of the truck: 'Baagh Bhaee Bandhu'. It was written in Hindi, but Darsha didn't know much Hindi.

As the truck pulled away, Darsha ran home to her mum and dad.

"Mum!" she yelled. "Mum, I need your help! What does Baagh Bhaee Bandhu mean?"

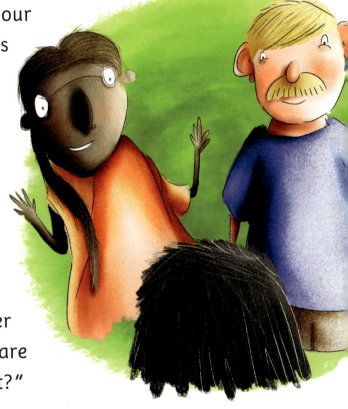

"Calm down Darsha!" giggled her mum. "It means The Tiger Brothers. Why are you asking that?"

Darsha explained her crazy day. Then she explained that she wanted to find the tiger. Darsha's mum didn't feel like giggling anymore.

"Are you crazy?" asked Darsha's mum. Darsha's dad didn't know what to say.

"NO!" cried Darsha. "The tiger was friendly, and I want to see it again!"

"Tigers hurt people, Darsha! Don't be so silly. Go to your room and calm down," said Darsha's dad. Darsha stamped her way down the hall.

She had to see the tiger again. She logged onto her computer, typed in 'Baagh Bhaee Bandhu' and tracked down the address. It wasn't far. Darsha slid back the window. She looked back to the bedroom door. Her parents weren't going to like this.

Soon enough, The Tiger Brothers' sign came into view. The moonlight lit the building up just enough for Darsha to find her way around the back. Tall metal bars jetted up into the air, keeping her from getting in.

Something rustled in the bush. Two eyes pierced through the leaves.

"Hello?" quivered Darsha. A rumbling growl grew deeper and stronger, and a slow tapping of paws turned into a gallop. The tiger ran and roared at the cage.

Darsha closed her eyes. Her heart was racing. Then, the roaring stopped. Darsha opened her left eye slowly, followed by her right. The tiger was leaning forward, as if it knew who Darsha was.

Darsha took a step forward, and the tiger jumped back and forth. Its eyes grew wider and filled up with excitement. It ran in circles and bounced around. They played through the bars until the Sun began to rise and Darsha had to leave.

Over the nights that followed, Darsha kept returning to see the tiger. She called the tiger Aditi, which meant 'freedom'. She showed Aditi her paper models, including her most recent creation – a tiger. Darsha and Aditi were becoming the best of friends.

One night was not like the others, though. Darsha sat by the bars on her own all night. Aditi never came to see her.

In fact, Aditi had gone altogether.

Chapter Four

Three Years Later

"HAPPY BIRTHDAY!" everyone cheered. Darsha loved birthdays. Being nine was going to be tough, though. It wasn't far off being a teenager and that wasn't far off being a grown-up, and nobody wants to be one of those. Darsha's dad had a surprise for her.

Her parents packed the car and off they went. All the excitement had made Darsha sleepy. Her head bounced on the seatbelt as the car bumbled over holes in the road.

"Darsha... we're here," said her dad softly. Darsha didn't wake up. "DARSHA!" he grunted as Darsha jumped a little off her seat. She peeped through the window and read the sign: 'West Bengal Zoo'.

However, rather than feeling happy and excited, Darsha looked a little sad.

"Are you OK, Darsha?" her Mum asked.

"Yes," said Darsha. "It's just that this reminds me of Aditi. I miss her." It had been three years since Aditi disappeared.

Darsha tried to smile. She didn't want to be sad for her birthday surprise. The West Bengal Zoo had so much to look at. There were black bears, huge tortoises, scary lions, giant anteaters and...

"Bengal tigers," said Darsha, reading from the sign. "Aditi was a Bengal tiger." She felt sad again.

Darsha went and sat beside the window. She pulled out her tiger model. While she was setting up the model, a tiger had wandered up to the glass. It seemed interested in Darsha's model.

Darsha's eyes grew wider. "Aditi?" she muttered. The tiger stood up and roared. Suddenly the tiger was much less friendly.

Darsha screamed and her parents held her tightly. She turned back to see another tiger approaching. Its slow tapping of paws turned into a gallop. The second tiger ran and roared at the first, scaring it away.

It pressed its nose to the glass, looking at Darsha and then at the model tiger. Excitement filled its eyes, before it started jumping around...

"ADITI!"

Chapter Five

The Distraction

Darsha pressed her button nose up against the glass window, and the tiger did the same. These eyes had met twice before. Darsha and Aditi had found each other again. They played through the glass just like best friends, while Darsha's parents watched on.

"I told you! I told you three years ago that Aditi was gentle and kind! We could have saved her back then, but you wouldn't let me see her!" shouted Darsha. A tear fell from her eye. "I won't lose her to a cage twice. Help me free her, please!"

"No! It's too dangerous!" Darsha's dad said firmly. "Isn't that right?" he said to Darsha's mum.

Except, Darsha's mum had gone.

Several pigs and sheep charged past Darsha and her dad, followed by lots of zookeepers and Darsha's mum. She knelt down beside Darsha.

"Don't ask questions," she whispered in Darsha's ear. "Unlatch the gate and use the back exit. The keepers will be busy for a while." Darsha's eyes lit up. "And Darsha... please, be safe."

"Aditi, come with me," Darsha whispered through the glass before running around the side of the enclosure.

"What did you say to her?!" yelped Darsha's dad.

Aditi followed Darsha to the back gate. Darsha's heart started beating faster. What if Aditi wasn't safe after all? Questions swirled around Darsha's head. She squeezed her eyes shut and pulled the latch across, opening the gate.

Very slowly, Aditi moved towards Darsha, who was frozen still. The last two times Aditi was this close to a human, she lost her family and got shot with a dart. But that didn't stop her this time.

She leapt on Darsha and brushed her head on hers, like a big ginger tabby cat.

Chapter Six

Two Tigers on a Shelf

As the last part of the Sun set in the sky, Darsha and Aditi arrived at the edge of the forest Aditi once left. Aditi's legs were shaking. She took a few nervous steps before looking back to Darsha.

"It's OK, Aditi. This is your home, remember?" said Darsha.

Aditi didn't relax, but Darsha had an idea. She slowly led Aditi back into the forest and started gathering plants. She placed them on the floor in the shape of a pillow. Darsha laid down and rested her head, and Aditi laid beside her.

"I'll stay here until morning," Darsha said.

Two things woke Darsha up the next day. One was the bright sunrise. The other was a deep growl. Darsha blinked. A set of sharp teeth greeted her. She called for Aditi as a tiger came closer, but Aditi was gone. The tiger's eyes met hers, and Darsha noticed something odd. This tiger had a large, round patch of black fur around its eye.

Another growl came from behind Darsha. Aditi was back. The two tigers let out fierce roars and paced around each other. Then, very suddenly, they stopped. Everything fell silent and still.

Aditi pounced on the other tiger. They rolled around, but didn't seem to be fighting. They seemed to know each other. They seemed to be family.

Four days later...

Humans and tigers were never supposed to be friends. But somehow, Darsha managed to make friends with one like no one had ever done before. Darsha lived up to her name, and really did make great things happen. Aditi was happy and free, and back with her family in the forest.

Darsha was making another model. It was another paper tiger.

Fold by fold, she carefully finished it that night. Then she coloured a large black patch on its eye. She put it up on her bedroom shelf, right beside the other tiger, where they stayed together forever.

Great Things

1. What were the two colours of paper Darsha was looking at in the shop?
   (a) Green and Purple
   (b) Green and Orange
   (c) Orange and Purple

2. What was the name of the zoo that Darsha's family visited?

3. Aditi was taken away from Darsha twice in this story. How do you think Darsha felt when she finally rescued Aditi? Have you ever felt this way?

4. Why do you think Darsha's mum helped her to free Aditi?

5. Aditi met another tiger at the end of the story. Where have you seen this tiger before, and how does Aditi know the other tiger?

©2021 **BookLife Publishing Ltd.**
King's Lynn, Norfolk PE30 4LS

ISBN 978-1-83927-435-0

All rights reserved. Printed in Malaysia.
A catalogue record for this book is available from the British Library.

Great Things
Written by William Anthony
Illustrated by Drue Rintoul

An Introduction to BookLife Readers...

Our Readers have been specifically created in line with the London Institute of Education's approach to book banding and are phonetically decodable and ordered to support each phase of Letters and Sounds.

Each book has been created to provide the best possible reading and learning experience. Our aim is to share our love of books with children, providing both emerging readers and prolific page-turners with beautiful books that are guaranteed to provoke interest and learning, regardless of ability.

BOOK BAND GRADED using the Institute of Education's approach to levelling.

PHONETICALLY DECODABLE supporting each phase of Letters and Sounds.

EXERCISES AND QUESTIONS to offer reinforcement and to ascertain comprehension.

BEAUTIFULLY ILLUSTRATED to inspire and provoke engagement, providing a variety of styles for the reader to enjoy whilst reading through the series.

AUTHOR INSIGHT:
WILLIAM ANTHONY

Despite his young age, William Anthony's involvement with children's education is quite extensive. He has written over 60 titles with BookLife Publishing so far, across a wide range of subjects. William graduated from Cardiff University with a 1st Class BA (Hons) in Journalism, Media and Culture, creating an app and a TV series, among other things, during his time there.

William Anthony has also produced work for the Prince's Trust, a charity created by HRH The Prince of Wales that helps young people with their professional future. He has created animated videos for a children's education company that works closely with the charity.

This book focuses on developing independence, fluency and comprehension. It is a white level 10 book band.